What they're saying about Ann Kelly's
Feeling NAKED on the FIRST TEE

Often ranked #1 'golf for women'
amazon.com

"...superbly covers equipment, terms, simplified rules, speed of play and many other need-to-know items."
Alan Gossman, **The Island Golfer**

"...countless essential items for the new golfer."
Golf Business (National Golf Course Owners Association)

"Ladies, you'll love this book."
Chris Rowsell, **The Calgary Sun** columnist

"...thank you for your little pink book. I plan on supplying my students with their very own copies."
Susan Briske, LPGA Teaching Professional, California

"This book will definitely help new golfers."
R.J. Lancaster, President, Golf Education and Learning Institute, Phoenix, AZ. Guest Lecturer, San Diego Golf Academy, Arizona Campus

"Don't start golf without it!"
Golf West Magazine (Pacific Northwest)

Feeling NAKED on the FIRST TEE

An Essential Guide
for New Women Golfers

Feeling NAKED on the FIRST TEE

An Essential Guide for New Women Golfers
by Ann Kelly

GA KELLY PUBLISHING

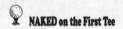
Canadian Cataloguing in Publication Data

Kelly, Ann

Feeling Naked on the First Tee: An essential guide for new women golfers

ISBN 978-0-9686289-2-8

1. Golf for women. I. Title.

— PREVIOUS (FIRST) EDITION —

First printing 1999. 2nd (rev.), 3rd: 2000. 4th (rev.), 5th: 2001.
6th, 7th: 2002. 8th (rev), 9th, 10th: 2003. 11th: 2004. 12th, 13th: 2005.
14th, 15th: 2006. 16th, 17th, 18th: 2007. 19th: 2008.
20th, 21st (rev.): 2009. 22nd: 2010. 23rd: 2011. 24th: 2012.
25th: 2016. 26th: 2017. 27th (rev.): 2019.

© Ann Kelly 1999–2019

Translations: Icelandic 2007; Chinese 2015; Estonian 2019

Congratulations, you have purchased a 'green' book!
Using light-weight paper, this edition is 1/2 the weight
and 1/2 the thickness of the original.
However, none of the valuable information has been omitted.

Contents

Contents

DEDICATION

To my father, Ted Wilson,
who loved the game and
at 86, died on the golf course
after parring the 17th Hole.

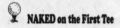

Acknowledgements

A S YOU WILL SEE, I've had lots of help and encouragement from many friends and relatives to get this guide to the printer! In the initial stages Rose MacAllister and my sister-in-law Barbara Campbell formed the rooting section. Early inspiration also came from R.J. Lancaster, the author of *Top 40 Things that Considerate Golfers Do.* The numbers swelled as Carolyn Levesque, Barb Young, Pat Nichol and Bernie Neufeld formed a working round table for critical input from new golfers.

The material was kindly and critically read by Tina James, Dorothy Clark, Sylvia Hoenson, Gladys Lord, Ramona Lumpkin, Marg and Murray Arnold and my dear sister Jane Davidson. Noel Richardson and Al Frame lent me their enthusiasm.

Thanks also go to the Vancouver Island professionals at Cordova Bay Golf Course, Jim Goddard and Todd Mahovlich, and to Dale Broughton, a professional at Blenkinsop Valley Golf Center who not only had the courage to adjust my swing but who also lent me his expertise. I am grateful for the encouragement from 'Stormin' Norm' Jackson, the

 NAKED on the First Tee

professional at Cowichan Golf and Country Club and also for
the insight of Larry Gray who captured many golfers' true
feelings when he coined the name, *Naked on the First Tee*.

Family support was very significant as my children Sarah and
Craig gave me a perspective from the younger generation of
golfers, and my husband Gerry, a very patient teacher on the
golf course whose home office I have turned upside down,
was my major soul-mate and advocate.

I am most grateful to Miriam MacPhail and Soren Henrich
who have been invaluable in the design and illustration
of this guide.

Feeling NAKED
An Essential Guide for New Women Golfers
on the FIRST TEE

What should I wear?

How can I get started?

Why do golfers need so many golf clubs?

What does "par" mean?

Why are "tee times" at such peculiar times?

These are just a few of the questions that people new to the game of golf are asking.

This wonderful guide is for new woman golfers. It includes a broad overview of a golf course, the game of golf, how to get started, the etiquette of golf (often unwritten but essential) and countless other "need-to-know" items. The aim of this guide is to create an awareness of the game of golf. It is mainly to help new golfers feel more comfortable on the golf course and <u>NOT</u> **Naked on the First Tee!**

There is a lot of material in this guide. Don't panic! You'll catch on quickly.

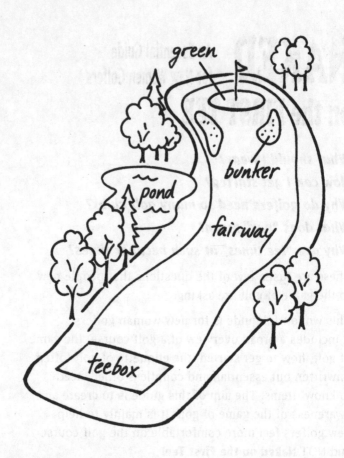

The Golf Course:
key elements of a hole

Each hole on a golf course has the same key elements, but differs in layout and distance from Tee Box to Green.

The Game

The regulation game of golf consists of 18 holes.
New golfers often start by playing 9 hole courses
which should take approximately 2 hours

Each hole consists of a Tee Box, the Fairway, and the Green

○ The **Tee Box**: a short patch of grass from where
everyone starts. All courses have a series of different
starting tees depending on your ability. The new
golfer will usually start at the forward tee, the one
closest to the fairway.

○ The **Fairway**: a stretch of mowed grass which is often
lined by trees, bushes,(ugh), patches of sand called
bunkers, or scenic lakes or ponds. (Not very scenic
when your ball lands in them!)

○ The **Green**: a very short carefully groomed patch of
grass where there is a flagstick in a hole.

The objective of the game of golf is to hit your ball from
the tee box, along the fairway and finally into the hole on
the green with the fewest strokes (hits) possible. Sounds
simple, doesn't it!

What Do I Need?

Golf Clubs

There are many combinations of golf clubs which players may have in their bags. Each club is designed to hit the ball a certain height and travel a certain distance.

○ **Woods:** #1 (driver), #3, #5, #7, #9, #11
These woods have fat heads and were originally made of wood, but now are made of many types of space age materials!

wood

○ **Hybrids:** #2, #3, #4, #5, #6
These clubs look like a 'fat iron';
also known as 'Rescue' or 'Utility' clubs.

hybrid

○ **Irons:** #3, #4, #5, #6, #7, #8, #9

○ **Wedges:** Pitching, Sand, Lob, Approach

○ **Putter**

iron

A typical bag of clubs could include

1–2 Woods	1 Pitching Wedge (PW)
1–2 Hybrids	1 Sand Wedge (SW)
7 Irons	1 Putter

putter

Clubs get longer as their numbers decrease, from the #9 iron to the driver. As well, the loft/angle of the blade decreases with the club number.

What does all this mean? Just this...a short club (for instance, a #9) is designed to hit the ball high and a short distance. A long club will hit the ball lower and will travel a longer distance.

9-iron ← → 3-iron

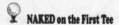
After several practice sessions you will have a better idea what distance you will get from hitting the different clubs. It is a good idea to create a **Cheat Sheet** (showing the distance you hit with each of your clubs) which you could attach to your bag. *(See page 18–19)*

While casual play has no restrictions, tournament play requires that a player not carry more than 14 clubs.

 New golfers sometimes start playing with irons only. They often don't use a driver — they may use a #3 wood or #5 wood off the tee box instead. There is little reason for a beginner to carry around 14 clubs. You can add clubs to your bag as you become comfortable using them.

New technology and new materials, along with golfers who are continually seeking more distance and accuracy, give rise to many new clubs each year. As well, golfers are looking for clubs they feel are easier to hit. Some types of newer clubs you will hear about are: rescue clubs, hybrid clubs and a variety of wedges.

Purchasing Golf Clubs

You don't necessarily need new clubs to start. You could check the classified ads but have an experienced golfer accompany you to check out used clubs. If you do purchase used clubs it is a good idea to replace the grips that probably have become very slippery. Any Pro Shop can do this for between $5.00 and $10.00 per club.

When you are ready to invest in a set of golf clubs, go to the local certified golf professional or a reputable golf store and seek their help. Most golf shops have either a hitting cage (a net) in the store or a driving range close at hand. You will be able to try out clubs made by several different manufacturers.

Clubs vary widely in feel, sound, and appearance and, yes, there is a difference that will be important to your game. How to choose? Simply put – the clubs that "look and feel right' are likely the ones for you!

Heed the advice of the professionals.

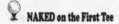

Golf Bag

○ The lighter the bag the better, as it often gets heavier as the game progresses – due to golfer fatigue that is!

○ Make sure that the zippers remain closed as it is easy to be dropping items (like your car keys) as you go along. Also, if the zippers are left gaping open, they may have a tendency to break, or the crows and squirrels may steal your goodies!

Balls

○ New balls are nice but not necessary! Good used (experienced) balls are available in Pro Shops.

○ Avoid balls that look as if they've been hit too many times, are cut or badly marked, or appear stained from sitting in a creek for too long.

○ Golf balls come in many colours and in different compressions/hardnesses. The softer the ball, the easier it is to hit – that's the theory anyway!

○ Balls are numbered for identification – often from 1 to 8. Remember and tell your playing partners the make and the number of your ball (it is a 2 stroke penalty if you hit another player's ball).

○ Some golfers use
a felt marker to put an
identifying mark on
their ball.

Towel

Golf towels are used to
clean the dirt and sand off clubs,
wipe your hands, or your brow! On the
green, when you are able to pick up your ball
after having marked it, you should clean the
ball so it will have a 'true' roll when you putt.

Umbrella

Golf umbrellas are generally large and do a respectable
job of keeping you dry if a sudden shower makes an
appearance. It's suggested that you choose one with a
wooden or graphite shaft, as a metal shaft could conduct
electricity in a lightning storm.

Essential accessories

Tees, ball markers, repair tool, pencil, sun screen, bug spray, feminine products, aspirin, bandaid, credit card, $2 – $5, lipstick, comb, energy source (power bar*), water bottle.

Often women carry a little zippered bag that they are able to attach to their golf bag in which they can put most of the above items. And if you don't need any of the items in your kit, you can be sure that others in your group may.

(There is no expectation that you will share your food with others.)

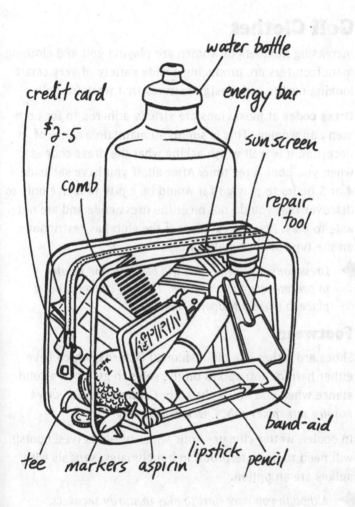

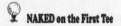
Golf Clothes

Increasing numbers of women are playing golf and clothing manufacturers are producing a wide variety of very smart looking outfits with design features that work for golf.

Dress codes at most clubs are strictly adhered to for both men and women. This is simply to maintain a sense of decorum. It is well worth asking what the dress code is when you book a tee time. After all, if you have set aside 4 or 5 hours to play golf it would be a pity to arrive only to discover that you do not meet the dress code and are not able to play. Also check to see if the club has restrictions on the type of shoe spikes worn.

 Dress conservatively – you will blend in and be able to concentrate on your game. The golf course is not a place to make a fashion statement.

Footwear

Shoes are rather like old-fashioned Oxfords, which have either hard or soft spikes on the soles to give you a solid stance when you swing the club. ***Caution****: many courses require soft spikes only. Check beforehand!*

In cooler, wetter climates your shoes or boots (yes! boots!) will need to be waterproof. In hot climates, sandals with spikes are an option.

 Although you may start to play in sturdy sneakers, golf shoes are mandatory at many clubs.

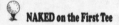
Tops

O Should be easy fitting, with a collar and/or sleeves.

O Any logos should be small and discreet.

O Colour is important only as it applies to the weather: a black or navy top worn on a hot day will absorb the sun's rays and may not be very comfortable.

Bottoms

Lots of choices here:

O slacks, Capri pants, shorts, skorts and skirts; length of shorts, skorts and skirts: just above the knee;

O should be comfortable enough for wearing for 5 hours of walking, bending and stretching;

O should have deep, easily-accessible pockets on both sides.

> *Don't even* *think* *of denim* *at most* *courses!*
>
>

Socks

Ankle to knee length – usually depends on the weather.

Rain/Cold weather gear

Be ready with a light sweater and/or water resistant jacket in your bag... if the rain appears you will likely be at the farthest point of the course from the clubhouse or your car! A jacket should "breathe', be a soft quiet fabric, and allow you to swing freely.

Glove

Generally most players wear one golf glove that helps in gripping the club. If you are right-handed the glove goes on the left hand, and vice-versa for lefties. Both leather or synthetic all-weather gloves are available.

Hat/Visor

Offers good protection from the sun; as well, the brim can help cut down the distraction of extraneous movement around you and give you better focus on the ball.

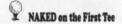

Lessons, Lessons, Lessons

Golf is a game where you take

> a very long stick to hit
>
> a very little ball a desired distance and finally into
>
> a very small hole!

It cannot be stressed strongly enough that lessons from a qualified professional will give you a good start to the game.

You will learn how to stand, how to grip the club, and the many parts to a good swing that will enable you to hit the little ball! This will take some time, so please be patient!

 Although it may be helpful at first, DO NOT rely on friends or spouse to help you get better at this game.

Where will I go for lessons?

○ Private lessons at a golf course or driving range usually last ½ hour and cost from $30 to $50. They often come in 3- or 4-lesson packages.

○ Group lessons are often given at golf courses, driving ranges, the local community college or through recreation programs.

○ **All lessons should be interspersed with practice sessions at a driving range. You will be surprised at how quickly you can improve!**

The Driving Range

The term 'driving range' is a misnomer, because golfers use the range for practising with all clubs in their bag, not just their drivers! Perhaps it should be named the **Practice Range**!

○ If you do not own a set of clubs, phone the driving range and ask if they have rentals available.

○ Mimic the conditions under which you will play. Dress appropriately and wear your golf shoes.

○ Pay for a bucket of practice balls at the counter. You may be given a token to use at the ball machine where you will retrieve your bucket of balls. (Place your bucket correctly before inserting your token or a small avalanche of balls will very quickly litter the ground at your feet!)

○ Find an empty stall, set your equipment down, take several warm-up stretches and swings before starting to hit balls.

○ Always give other golfers a wide berth when passing them! A club can maim!

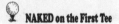

A recommended routine at the driving range is to start with your #9 iron and several nice easy swings. After several successful hits you can move to your # 7 iron, followed by #5 iron, #5 wood, #3 wood. Finally when you are nicely warmed up you are ready to use your driver. Save a few balls for a couple of easy swings with a #9 at the end of the session.

Stop when you get tired!!!

 Remember to visit the putting and chipping areas — this is where you can really cut strokes off your score!

The Cheat Sheet

The practice range is an ideal location to create a **Cheat Sheet** for yourself which would tell you the approximate distances that you can hit the ball with your different clubs. You could then put it into a small plastic sleeve, or laminate it, and attach it to your golf bag for quick reference.

Driving (Practice) Range

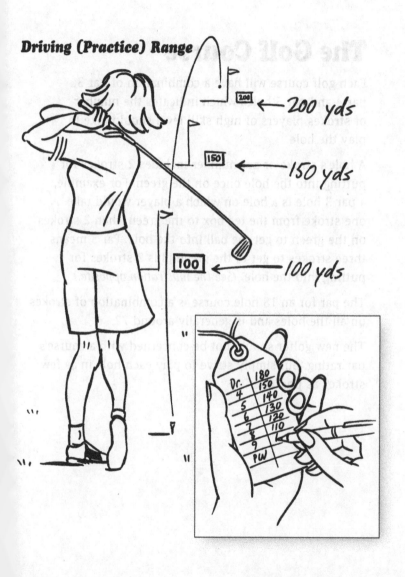

200 yds

150 yds

100 yds

Dr.	180
4	150
5	140
6	130
7	120
8	110
9	
PW	

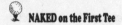

The Golf Course

Each golf course will have a combination of par 3, par 4 and par 5 holes which indicates the number of strokes players of high skill level should take to play the hole.

A hole's stroke or par number includes 2 strokes for putting into the hole once on the green. For example, a par 3 hole is a hole on which a player would take one stroke from the tee box to the green, then 2 strokes on the green to get the ball into the hole. Par 5 means three strokes to get to the green plus 2 strokes for putting into the hole. *(See the illustration opposite.)*

The par for an 18 hole course is a combination of strokes on all the holes and is generally around 72.

The new golfer should not be concerned with a course's par rating, but simply strive to play each hole in as few strokes as possible.

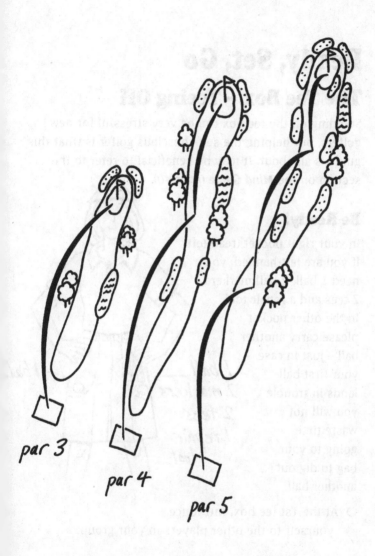

par 3

par 4

par 5

Ready, Set, Go

The Tee Box – Teeing Off

Standing on the tee box can be very stressful for new golfers, but helping the self-conscious golfer is what this guide is all about. It may be beneficial to refer to the section on the **Mind Game** *(page 40)*.

Be Ready!

In your right pocket (read left if you are left-handed) you need 1 ball, 2 ball markers 2 tees and a repair tool. In the other pocket please carry another ball – just in case your first ball lands in trouble you will not waste time going to your bag to dig out another ball.

1 ball →
2 markers
2 tees
1 repair tool

← *1 bal.*

○ At the 1st tee box, introduce yourself to the other players in your group.

○ You may wish to loosen up by taking a couple of practice swings to the side of the tee box. Make sure you are a good distance from your fellow players. A golf club can do a lot of damage!

○ The Tee Box usually has 4 or 5 sets of different coloured markers between which the ball is placed. Beginning golfers usually use the ones furthest forward.

○ "Ready golf" is a term often used on the tee box – it simply means the person who is ready can step up and hit their ball. It is a way to speed up play.

○ Stand at least 12 -15 feet from a player who is getting ready to hit. **Be silent and still**. Whispering is disconcerting and even scratching your nose can be distracting.

○ When it is your turn, place your ball o a tee between or behind the forward tee-markers. The easiest and most efficient way to do this is with the ball in the palm of your hand and the tee between your index and middle finger as in the illustration. You then can use the ball to push the tee into the ground.

○ The tee box is the only place you are able to place your ball on a tee.

○ The first shot is often the most nerve racking one – that "naked feeling". To help, players often use their favorite club.

"Take a Mulligan."

This is a second attempt on a first shot, usually on the first hole. It is illegal, but often used in a friendly social game.

○ One practice swing is considered sufficient and will do minimal damage to the tee box. Swing smoothly!

○ Watch to see where your ball lands! If you cannot follow it to its final resting place, choose a tree or bush in the direction the ball was heading and head in that direction, once all players have hit.

○ Once all players have hit...the game has begun! Everyone goes smartly to their ball and prepares to hit a second shot.

The Fairway

Hopefully your ball is still on the 'short grass' – or the fairway. If not, see *Hazards, page 28.*

○ Be aware of the yardage from your ball to the flagstick. The 150-yards markers are often on both sides of the fairway. These could be stakes, bushes, or special trees. Other yardages are often marked on the fairway by tags on the sprinkler heads. These distances are marked to the center of the green. Know which club you will need for the desired distance. *(Refer to your Cheat Sheet – page 18–19)*

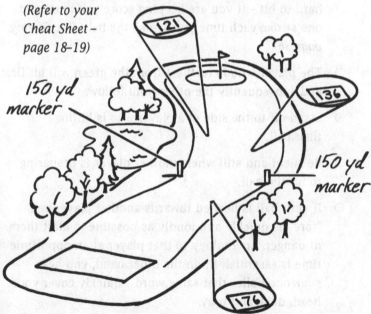

150 yd marker

150 yd marker

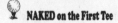
○ Bring your clubs close to where your ball lies; leave them off to the side and out of the way of your swing. This saves time as you will not have to walk back to pick them up.

○ Go to your ball and determine which club to use so you're ready to play when it's your turn.

○ Do not pick up or otherwise touch your ball until you reach the green; however, if you are a beginner in a social game, most players will not object if you move it with your club out of a situation which you find hard to hit – if you are keeping score you must add one stroke each time you stroke the ball. *(See Scoring, page 36)*.

○ The player who is furthest from the green will hit first and subsequently the others will follow.

○ Stand off to the side of a player who is hitting their ball.

○ Be silent and still when another player is preparing to hit the ball.

○ If your ball is headed towards another player yell "fore" as quickly and loudly as possible to alert them of danger. An apology to that player at an opportune time is essential. If, on the other hand, you hear someone holler that same word...quickly cover your head, duck and pray.

○ If you have created a divot (hole) and sent a small
patch of grass flying when you made your shot...
retrieve and replace the grass and tamp it down
with your foot. Alternatively, a sand/seed/fertilizer
combination may be provided to fill the hole.

A LL GOLFERS HAVE DAYS/HOLES when they struggle
and their swing does not seem to be working.
This can become tiring and discouraging.
    When this is you... just pick your ball up
after 5–6 hits, take it to the green and putt with the
others. To continue to "dribble" down the fairway
may upset the concentration of others in your
group and slow down the play.
    Remember, it's only a game, so settle yourself
down and get ready for the next hole.

Could be Trouble! ~ Lost Balls

Trees, bushes and long grass...

Lost a ball? Look quickly: if you can't find it within two minutes, drop another ball from your bag and add two strokes to your score. *(Get balls on sale whenever possible!)*

Could be More Trouble! ~ Hazards

Water

○ Good players do not worry about the water on the course, but it is very daunting for the beginner and seems magnetic. Visualise where you want the ball to end up, focus on the ball, keep your head down as you swing smoothly and the ball will go up and over!

○ If you have hit your ball into the water and can see it...use a retriever (a long pole with a scoop), then drop the ball and add 1 stroke. *(See Rules, page 34)*

○ If you cannot retrieve your ball from the water, kiss it goodbye, drop another at the point where it entered the water, and hit away – add 1 stroke.
(See Rules, page 34)

③ *Hurrah!*

② *Drop retrieved or replacement ball here*

① *Oops! into the water!*

Bunker

○ The shot from the bunker/sand often can be very intimidating so it is worth practising before you make your debut on the golf course.

○ You are not allowed to touch the sand with your club ("ground your club") before you hit the ball.

○ You may clean up any debris, such as leaves or twigs in the sand trap before you hit the ball.

○ After you have successfully hit the ball out of the trap you must use the rake and smooth the sand for the following players – very much like other household chores I'm afraid.

○ If you have tried to hit your ball a couple of times and are no further along – please toss the ball out of the sand, rake the trap and continue.

Rakes

The placement of rakes has always amused me. There are so many, and often complex, rules in the game of golf... but the one thing that cannot be decided on is the placement of the rakes. In, or out of the bunker? Simply put the rake back where you found it!

Putting ~ The Green

Hurrah! You've reached the Green!

leave golf bags here

next tee

○ Think ahead as you approach the green and locate the direction of the next tee box.

○ Leave your clubs between the green and the path to the next tee box. This is important as your clubs can easily be picked up

direction of play

on the way to the next tee box. You will not waste time going back to the front of the green and you will not annoy following golfers who are approaching the green.

○ Once all balls are on the green, everyone should mark their ball* (the little disc marker that is in your pocket is placed, without touching the ball, directly behind the ball, after which the ball is picked up).

---

* To replace a ball that has been marked, reverse the procedure: place the ball directly in front of the marker then pick up the marker.

The player who is closest to the flagstick takes it out of the hole and places it on the ground so it is out of the way of any ball being putted.

○ Avoid stepping on the 'line' of others' putts. Your footprint can cause the ball to go off course.

○ The person whose ball is furthest from the hole putts first – if that ball does not go into the hole that player can either continue putting or can mark the ball in the new position. The next player to putt is now the farthest away from the hole – and so it goes until everyone has putted into the hole.

○ To speed up play, a putt very close to the hole may be called a "gimme" or players may say "it's yours"; then you can pick the ball up and count the pick-up as one stroke.

"Drive for show, putt for dough."

Putting is often more important than driving.

○ **Tending the flagstick**
If a player is unable to see the hole because of
distance from the hole or undulation of the green
another person may "tend" the flagstick. That person
stands out to the side of the flagstick with one hand
on the flagstick ready to
pull it out and let the
ball drop. Make sure
that your shadow
does not cover
the hole.

 *Once your ball is in the
hole, retrieve it **immediately;** golfers are very
superstitious and believe
that there is only room
for one ball in the hole!*

(note shadow
does not cover
the hole)

○ When a player is putting

1. Be Silent and Still.

2. Do not distract by standing on
   an extension of a player's putt.

3. Do not cast your shadow on the line of their putt.

○ Use the repair tool in your pocket to repair the mark
your ball might have made as it landed on the green.
With a prying motion go around the ball mark pulling
the grass to the center, then tap it with your putter
to create a flat surface again.

○ Before leaving the green, check to see that no clubs are left behind. Laying extra clubs on the flagstick helps ensure that they aren't left behind.

○ Writing down the score on the score card is done on the next tee box.

Thanking your Playing Partners

At the end of the game vacate the green quickly. It is important etiquette to shake hands with all members of your group (yes, even your spouse) and thank them for the game.

> **"You have the honor."**
>
> *The person who scores the lowest on a given hole earns the right to tee up first on the next hole.*

Now, take your clubs to the storage area or your car before heading to the clubhouse ('the 19th hole') for a drink or a snack.

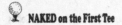

What Rules Should I Know?

There are lots of rules in this great game, but don't worry, you'll pick them up quickly and keep learning as you play.

It's also a good idea for a new golfer to 'fess up' and tell your fellow golfers that you may need help on some of the rules. However, to get you started...here are a couple of *simplified* rules.

○ Your ball must be played from behind the markers on the tee box until it drops into the hole on the green.

○ The ball must be played as it lies – sometimes this is not a pretty sight!

○ **Penalty Areas***

1. If your ball lands in a penalty area, you may take a practice swing, except in the bunker where you may not touch the sand ('ground your club') behind the ball.

2. If your ball lands in the water (marked by yellow stakes), quickly retrieve it if possible, or kiss it good-bye! and drop another ball behind the point of entry. Take one stroke penalty in either case.

3. If your ball lands in a lateral hazard (marked by red stakes) drop another ball within two club lengths of entry and no closer to the hole. Take a one stroke penalty.

○ Unplayable lies (this is when you can't get a decent swing at the ball, such as if it lies in a clump of bushes): you have three options, each with a one stroke penalty.

   1. Declare your ball "lost" and play from where you hit that last shot, or

   2. retrieve the ball and drop it within 2 club lengths, no closer to the hole, or

   3. retrieve the ball and drop it on an imaginary line from the unplayable lie through the flagstick. Go as far back as you wish.

○ **Lost ball**: If you think, after striking your ball, that your ball may be lost, immediately hit another ball (a provisional ball) which you will use if you are unable to find the first one. If you did not hit a 'provisional,' go back to the place where you hit your ball and hit another!

○ A ball ball must be dropped from knee height.*

When you start to play in a league, an official rule book is essential! ***Attend Rules Clinics whenever you get a chance!***

* ***NOTE:*** Some rules were changed in January 2019. See page 66 for some rules of interest to new golfers.

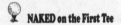

Scoring

When new golfers start to play, the scoring is often confusing and you may lose track of your shots easily – perhaps you are still taking considerably more shots than the others! There are several possible solutions for new golfers:

1. Don't count.

2. Count only excellent shots.

3. Count only the 'good' holes.

There are many devices that can be purchased to help you keep your score: beads, watches etc. As you improve, the number of shots you take on each hole will diminish and keeping track will be easier.

 Golf is a Game of Honour
Once you have decided to keep your score, it is imperative to be honest in recording your scores and to remember that you are playing against yourself. If you lose track or are confused about your score on a hole ask another player to quickly help you re-count it.

Golfers know that they are playing against the golf course and that the handicap system makes it fair to calculate the differences between golfers.

Scoring Terms

PAR	=	The defined number of strokes on a hole
Par minus 1 stroke	=	**BIRDIE**
Par minus 2 strokes	=	**EAGLE**
PAR + 1 stroke	=	**BOGEY** (ugh)
PAR + 2 strokes	=	**DOUBLE BOGEY** (ugh ugh)
PAR + 3 strokes	=	**TRIPLE BOGEY** (ugh ugh ugh)
Hole-in-One	=	A Miracle!

Handicap

This is a term you will hear often. It is an indicator of the skill level of the golfer.

An example – a person with a 20 handicap would, on average, score 92 (20 over par) on a par 72 course. The lower the handicap the better the golfer.

A person's handicap is set by a governing body and is established after several game scores have been recorded.

Player _____ **7** _____ Date _____

RATINGS	RED	WHITE	BLUE									
Men	68.1	69.6	71.0		Men	Amy	Sue	Pat	Alice **5**		Women	
Women	74.5	76.7	–									

	RED	WHITE	BLUE	PAR	HDCP	Amy	Sue	Pat	Alice		PAR	HDCP
1	367	382	397	4	11						4	7
2	364	374	408	4	9						4	11
3	389	396	420	4	1						5	3
4	150	154	155	3	13						3	15
5	486	506	515	5	5						5	1
6	396	403	429	4	3						5	9
7	126	149	160	3	17						3	17
8	322	322	327	4	15						4	13
9	366	385	405	4	7						4	5
OUT	2966	3071	3216	35							37	
10	404	415	430	4	4						5	14
11	163	209	237	3	14						3	16
12	409	416	423	4	2						5	6
13	334	346	386	4	12						4	4
14	418	463	494	5	10						5	2
15	145	157	157	3	18						3	18
16	369	379	385	4	8						4	8
17	365	382	400	4	16						4	12
18	341	396	414	4	6						4	10
IN	2948	3163	3326	35							37	
OUT	2966	3071	3216	35							37	
TOTAL	5912	6234	6542	70							74	
SIGNED: SCORER			**7**	HDCP				**8**			SIGNED: PLAYER	
				NET								

SLOPE RATING   MEN   RED: 124   WHITE: 127   BLUE: 130
WOMEN   RED: 135   WHITE: 140

Deciphering the Score Card

There are many forms of score cards, but though they may look different they still contain the same information.

1 Number of the hole

2 Yardage

3 PAR: the number of strokes an expert golfer is expected to score to complete a particular hole.

4 HDCP: Each hole is 'handicapped' as to its difficulty. For example, on this card, Men's hole #3 and Ladies' hole #5 are the most difficult on which to get par, and Men's hole #15 and Ladies' hole #15 is the easiest.

5 Area to record names. Scores will be recorded vertically under players' names.

6 PAR: the number of strokes an expert golfer is expected to score to complete this course.

7 Ratings which are important when it comes to comparing scores on different courses

8 Net score: the result of your score minus your handicap (*See Handicap, page 37*)

ATTENTION! *On the reverse side of a score card, there are often local rules pertaining to that specific course. Remember to read them – it may save you some strokes!*

The Mind Game

Your ball has just landed in the sand! And you say or think "Oh, I hate the sand!" This will probably guarantee that you will be in the sand a lot longer than you ever imagined.

Your ball is on the green 25 feet from the hole. You say or think "I'll never make it from here". And you won't!

Your "self-talk" or "self-think" is very important in the game of golf. These are the thoughts that you say to yourself on a continuous basis. It is important to be positive about the challenges you face on the golf course.

Some positive self-affirmations would be

> *I can hit this ball*
>
> *I can hit it out of the rough*
>
> *I love all my clubs*
>
> *I love the challenge of being in the sand*
>
> *I am a good putter*

Of course positive self-talk alone will not make you a better golfer. The combination of golf lessons, practice sessions, and positive self-talk however will give you a 1 – 2 – 3 punch and "a good leg up" on the game of golf!

Where Do I Play?

Golf Courses

Start by looking in the yellow pages or ask around!
Golf courses generally fall into the following categories.

Public Courses

Any golfer may phone and arrange tee times.

> **Par 3 Courses:** usually public with only short par 3
> holes – good to practice your short game!
> **Recommended for new golfers.**

> **Executive Courses:** These courses are shorter in
> length than a regulation 18 hole course.
> They can be either 9 or 18 holes. **Nine holes
> are recommended for new golfers.**

> **Regulation 18 Hole Course:** These courses are not
> recommended for new golfers. Once a player
> has reached a certain familiarity with golf skills,
> rules and etiquette, these courses will then
> provide 4 hours of challenge.

Semi-private Courses

Golfers may buy a membership which gives them the
privileges of private courses and a lower green fee than
non-members. Non-members may phone and book tee
times as well.

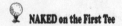

Private Courses

Generally an initial fee and a yearly membership fee
are required, which give you privileges of a locker, club
storage, club cleaning, shoe cleaning, and no green fees.
*Non-members would be only allowed as guests of a member
and a green fee will be charged.*

Tee times

To play golf you should reserve a 'tee time' at a particular
course.

To inquire if there is availability at a particular course,
phone the pro shop and the staff will assist you.

CHECKLIST
Things which are helpful to know in advance

Tee Time*
(You will be asked how many players, if any, will be with you.)

Green Fees	Credit cards accepted?	
Are power carts mandatory?	Suggested?	Cost
Are pull carts available?		Cost
What is the dress code for women?		
Is there a rain check policy?		
Directions to the course		
Anything else I should know before I arrive?		

**Tee times are 7/8/9 minutes apart and that's why you will be
given some seemingly peculiar times like 8:24 or 9:59.*

Arrive at the course **at least 30 minutes** ahead of your tee time and come dressed to play. This allows you to check in to the pro shop, pay your green fee, put your shoes on, and take a couple of practice putts on the putting green or hit some balls on the driving range.

Now... where do I put my purse? Only bring essential items to a golf course. Minimize what you need – perhaps your drivers license, a credit card and some money which, along with your car keys, you can put in a pocket on your golf bag.

Housekeeping Items

Most golf courses have a clubhouse that may include a restaurant, locker rooms, and a Pro Shop.

The Pro Shop is a small store that specializes in golf clothing, golf accessories and golf clubs. Tee times and golf lessons are also booked through the Pro Shop. This is where you will check in on arrival.

Washrooms are usually found in the clubhouse locker room, at the ninth hole, and discreetly hidden on the course. Ask where they are located before starting a round of golf!

Food, Glorious Food (Yes!) There could be a small restaurant in the clubhouse, a snack shack between the ninth and tenth hole, (here you must 'grab and run' unless

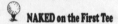

you want to lose your place to the following foursome) and a beverage cart on the course.

Warm-Up / Practice Facilities These could be a driving range, a putting green and a chipping area.

Can you tag along on a golf course? No, most courses strongly discourage or disallow persons walking on the course for safety reasons. Only playing golfers are allowed on most courses, and each golfer must have their own bag of golf clubs.

Weather Thunderstorms can be deadly on a golf course. If a storm with lightning is approaching, don't think you'll 'just finish playing the hole'. Leave the course immediately!

To Walk or To Ride ~ that is the question!

Walking

Some players prefer to carry their clubs – a light weight bag and a body that is in good shape are essential. Bags must be kept off the Tee Box, the Green, and the fringe around the green.

Pull carts These can be rented at most courses. Make sure that the bag is well anchored on the Pull Cart. It is easy to tip the whole cart when climbing a hill, or catch a wheel when crossing a bridge, and it is time-consuming (and messy) to gather everything up.

Riding

Power carts can be rented at most golf courses. Some courses require that you take a power cart due to the length, or terrain, of the course.

Power carts accommodate two people and the cost is usually shared. It is usually decided at the beginning who will do most of the driving and the driver's golf bag will be placed on the drivers side.

Be attentive to the noise of the cart when you are on the course so that you will not disturb others.

Often power carts must remain on the cart paths to

prevent damage to the course, especially after a heavy rain. Some courses will have a 90˚ Rule – this means that you must keep the cart on the cart path till you are adjacent to your ball, then turn 90˚ to get to the ball, hit the ball then return to the path.

Never pull or drive carts on the Tee Box or the Green. The course superintendent has worked very diligently to groom these areas.

Marshal (or Ranger/Player Assistant)

Treat the Marshal as a friend.

The duty of a Marshal, who patrols in a golf cart, is to help everyone on the course enjoy the game by keeping the pace steady and consistent. At any one time there could be over 100 other golfers on an 18 hole course. Most clubs want golfers to finish 18 holes of golf in 4 hours.

The Marshal also can assist with finding lost clubs or head covers, or deal with other groups around you which may be causing you concern.

If your group is playing slowly, the Marshal may ask your group to speed up or to let the group following you 'play through'. This means that your group will stand aside and let the following group play ahead of your group. Good golf etiquette means letting the group behind you play through even without the Marshal's request.

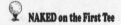
Speed of Play

○ Golfers will agree that keeping a good pace of play is very important.

○ Beginning golfers should have the ability to maintain a vigorous, steady pace.

○ Walk smartly on the course, or to and from your cart.

○ Golf is not a spectator game when you are a player.

○ You should be continually preparing for your next shot.

HINTS ON PICKING UP THE PACE	
○ Arm yourself with extra balls, tees and markers.	○ 'Hole out' or continuous putt.
○ Try to track everyone's shots – saves time looking for balls.	○ Line up your putt while others are putting – without disturbing anyone.
○ Take your bag to the ball, or take several clubs to the ball from a cart.	○ Be ready when it is your turn.
○ Think ahead and plan your next shot.	○ Keep up to the group <u>ahead</u> of you.
○ Play when ready as long as there is no danger to others.	○ After finishing a hole go directly to the next tee box before recording scores.

Ambience in your Group

The wonderful game of golf is a very self-centered game.
Other players are not concerned about how you are doing
yet they are very supportive. Your playing partners are
concerned about their next shot or still wondering about
their last shot! What is important to other players is your
awareness on the course, your ability to keep up the pace,
and your knowledge of the rules and etiquette.

○ Be aware whether the members of your group are
chatty or quiet and try and fit in.

○ Be cautious when telling others whether their shot
is good. It may be good from your point of view but
very poor for them. As well, if you haven't seen it
from their angle, you may be shouting *Good* when it
may be heading straight for the sand bunker or into
the lake!

○ Avoid giving advice to others unless asked.

○ Be cautious about asking for advice on your swing –
the practice range is the place to learn to adjust
a swing.

Attitude

○ Golfers of any skill level will enjoy playing with new golfers if those beginners know the etiquette and keep up with the pace of the group.

○ Remember that everyone on the course has set aside time and money to enjoy a game of golf. Be thoughtful of others by keeping up a good pace and keeping noise to a minimum.

○ Golf is a game of "pars and poors" and it can change from one day to the next, from one hole to the next and from one stroke to the next! It is not easy to stay upbeat and positive for several hours but reminding yourself to do so can help your game.

○ Try to relax – take several deep breaths, say a mantra, smile, whistle, or hum (to yourself, of course!).

○ Only about 15 minutes of a 4-hour round is spent actually swinging the golf club. Enjoy the other 3¾ hours. Enjoy the company of your playing partners and appreciate the serene and scenic surroundings.

"You don't have to play golf to relax, but you have to relax to play golf."

○ Women, golf is your game. It is ideally suited to your strengths. You don't have to be strong or tall or athletic. Skills such as patience, persistence, thoughtfulness, good decision making and problem solving, attention to detail, willingness to take instruction, and practice are very important in the game of golf. **So have fun and…Go For It!**

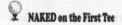

A Note on Tournaments

If you are asked to sign up for a tournament and your heart has just gone into a state of shock, the news may not be all bad. You will probably be placed on a team for most office and charity tournaments.

A common team format is the "scramble". Everyone on the four-person team takes their shot, walks up the fairway together and decides which one of the four shots is the best. The others then pick up their balls and play the next shot from that spot.

Another term that you may hear is "shotgun". This is where every team starts playing at the same time but on different holes of the course. Tournaments often use a shot gun start as everyone finishes at the same time. All players can then enjoy a meal together and perhaps a prize-giving ceremony.

To feel more comfortable when playing in a tournament, try to gain some experience on a golf course or at least spend a couple of sessions on the practice range before you willingly sign up. This will help ensure that your golfing day will be as fun and pleasant as possible.

Resources
Women's Leagues

Once you have mastered some of the skills of this game and know the rules and etiquette, there is a great deal of merit in joining a women's league.

Often Tuesday or Wednesday mornings are set aside for women's leagues; as well, in the early evenings there are business women's leagues.

You will have the opportunity of meeting new players, playing with players of similar ability and perhaps participating in skill and rules clinics scheduled especially for this group.

"This game is played between the ears."

The mental part of the game of golf is critical.

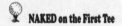

Plus...

The Golf Channel – Good for picking up helpful hints

Golf Tournaments on TV – more exposure to the game

Volunteering to assist in Golf Tournaments in your area

Monthly Golf Magazines for Women have excellent articles. As well there are a number of local publications that contain valuable information.

The Internet – this could keep you busy for hours!

A Mentor – a friend or acquaintance whom you could ask for help

Books, Video Tapes – lots of these items on the market. Visit any bookstore or golf store.

Warning!

New golfers are apt to fall in love with this
game! And on becoming members of this
million-member fraternity of golfers, they
should be prepared

O   to meet some wonderful people,

O   to spend time on some of the most
    beautiful properties on the planet,

O   to get out of bed to tee-off as the
    sun rises!

O   to have the car trunk filled with
    nothing but golf paraphernalia,

and perhaps most importantly,

O   to be on a continual quest for the
    perfect putter!

Oh what a wonderful game!

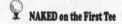

Golfers' Hints

○ "Arrive at the course at least 30 minutes before your tee time – try to hit some balls and relax!"

○ "Shoe polish and shoe trees are a good investment. They will substantially lengthen the life of your golf shoes. If you don't have a locker, put them in your trunk!"

○ "While tending the flagstick, grab the flag to stop it from flapping so it is not a distraction."

○ "Put the flagstick down on the green gently."

○ "Enter a sand bunker from the flattest area close to your ball." (and of course rake as you leave!)

○ "**Practise** on the driving/practice range, **play** on the golf course."

○ "If you are starting to watch golf on television – remember that you are seeing the best 10 or 12 players in the field of 150 or more. You are not seeing the others hit into the bushes, water or other hazards. So... set your sights accordingly and don't be so hard on yourself."

Appendix

And, if you dash off the golf course remembering that you are required to bring an item to a pot-luck, a bake-sale, the bridge group,... or you need a present for your child's teacher, I have a great recipe to share with you! It can be made from scratch and be out the door in less than 30 minutes. It is easy and delicious!

Kelly Krunch

2c flour	1c butter/margarine
1c white sugar	2 Tbsp instant coffee granules
1/2 tsp salt	1 tsp each vanilla & almond flavoring

Chocolate chips/sliced almonds *(optional)*

Pre-heat oven to 350°. Put all ingredients except chips/almonds into a large bowl. Mix with a pastry blender until everything is the size of peas. Spread onto a large cookie sheet, then sprinkle with chocolate chips and almonds and press them into the cookie base. Bake for 15–18 minutes, until edges start to brown. Let cool and crack into pieces.

While this is baking, practise your putting on the living room rug!

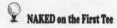

My Journal: How Am I Doing?

DATE	LOCATION	PARTNERS

SCORE	COMMENTS

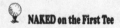

My Journal: How Am I Doing?

DATE	LOCATION	PARTNERS

SCORE	COMMENTS

Notes (or ... what I learned today!)

Must remember ...

- *keep up a good pace!*
- *BE SILENT and STILL*
  but breathe and enjoy!
- *place the ball marker directly behind the ball*
- *don't tread on other players' putting lines*
- *leave cart close to path going to next tee box*

✓ Leave plenty of time to get to golf course!

✓ Take time to check equipment before teeing off — don't assume it is all in order!

Notes

When asked to move my ball
marker on the green because it's in
the path of another player's ball, I
will flip my marker over to remind
me to remark before I putt!

Notes

....
....
....
....
....
....
....
....
....
....
....
....
....
....

Notes

. . . .

. . . .

. . . .

. . . .

. . . .

. . . .

. . . .

. . . .

. . . .

. . . .

. . . .

. . . .

. . . .

Changes to Rules of Golf
(January 2019)

Modernising the Rules of Golf begin in 2012, with goals of ensuring the Rules were easier to understand, making the game more appealing to newcomers, and increasing the pace of play.

Most of the Rules are unchanged, but some revisions you should pay attention to are:

○ Search time for the ball is now 3 minutes instead of 5.

○ If you accidently move a ball during a search, you may replace it.

○ If the ball is embedded in the 'general area', including in the semi-rough and rough, you may take a free drop.

○ When using a club to measure a ball's position, use your longest club (but not the putter).

○ When 'taking relief' (from an abnormal course condition or penalty area, for example), the ball must be dropped from knee height.

○ When a ball lands on the wrong green, you must drop and play it from outside the green.

○ If the ball accidently hits the player or his equipment, there is no penalty.

○ The club may touch the ground (be 'grounded') in the bunker, but not directly behind the ball.

- A double hit will only count as 1 stroke.

- You can move any loose impediments in the hazards; if the ball moves, it must be replaced.

- If the ball lands in a bunker, you have a new option of dropping the ball directly behind the bunker with a two-shot penalty.

- Water hazards are now called penalty areas, therefore you can take a sideways drop.

- Grounding the club in the penalty area is allowed.

- If, after the ball is marked on the green, it moves (such as by wind), it must be replaced with no penalty.

- If you move the ball accidently on the green, there is no penalty and you must replace the ball.

- All damage on the green may be repaired without penalty. This is not permission to smooth out your entire line of putt, as natural imperfections are part of the game.

- You cannot use your club to position yourself to putt.

- You are not allowed to have a caddy stand behind you on the green to help you line up the shot.

- The ball may hit the flagstick without penalty.

- If the ball is wedged in the cup between the stick and the edge of the cup, it is considered IN!

NOTE: Visit Yves Ton-That's site www.expertgolf.com for excellent information and videos.

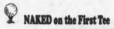

New Women Golfers...
a website just for YOU!

www.NewWomenGolfers.com

Questions about golf?
Rules-related or skills-related? Other?
This is the book for you!

Top Tips
Useful women's golf **Links**!
Book reviews and easy **ordering**!

Click in today...
www.NewWomenGolfers.com

We'd love to have you visit!

Helpful golf articles! on www.newwomengolfers.com

Avoid Common Mistakes

Making mistakes is an important part of learning how to play golf. However we do not want to embarrass ourselves and feel...

Charity Tournaments

Charity golf tournaments are extremely popular ways for non-profit organizations to raise money ... The players often get to play alongside local celebrities and expert golfers and there are prizes...

Improve! Easy Remedies!

It is no secret that Tiger Woods has spent hours on his workout routines and that VJ Singh spends hours on the practice range. Recreational golfers cannot afford the time to replicate the routines of the professionals but can easily improve their game by incorporating the...

Let's Speed Up Slow Play!

This article came to me from Christina Munro who was the Rules Chair, Zone 5 Women's Division, British Columbia, Canada. After years of observing groups on the golf course slowly losing sight of the group in front, she came up with this wonderful...

Read more about the above topics (and many others)... go to www.newwomengolfers.com

About the Author

Ann Kelly refers to herself as an average golfer who summoned up her courage to play the game of golf after her two children left for university. Now she's hooked! A background in teaching Physical Education, and later training women to re-enter the workforce, honed her sensitivity as to why women feel "naked on the first tee".

Playing on courses in North America, Europe and "down under", she noticed that women have a universal self-consciousness, not just about hitting the ball, but how to behave on the golf course. This guide was written to help new women golfers quickly understand the unwritten, and often unspoken nuances in the game of golf, and feel comfortable and knowledgeable on the golf course.

Ann has been a member of the Edmonton Country Club (Alberta) where she was also on the organizing committee for the LPGA duMaurier Classic. She is a member of the Royal Colwood Golf Club located in Victoria, British Columbia, Canada.

Do you have additional hints for new women golfers?
Visit my website **www.newwomengolfers.com** for useful tips and answers to frequently-asked questions.Write to me: Ann Kelly, #132, 883 Van Isle Way, Victoria, BC Canada V9B 5R8. Email me at ann.kelly@shaw.ca .

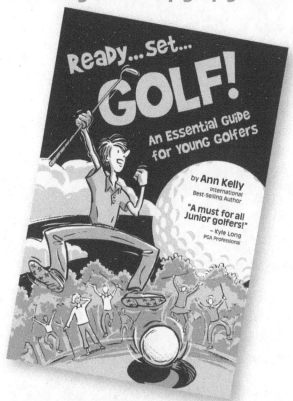

CPSIA information can be obtained
at www.ICGtesting.com
Printed in the USA
BVHW072208301122
653183BV00025B/288